THE BIG BIG BIG BIG BOAT!

And other **Bible Stories** about

OBEDIENCE

By Christine Harder Tangvald

Illustrated by Patrick Girouard

Chariot Books™
David C. Cook Publishing Co

CONTENTS

Chariot Books™ is an imprint of David C. Cook Publishing Co.
David C. Cook Publishing Co., Elgin, Illinois 60120
David C. Cook Publishing Co., Weston, Ontario
Nova Distribution Ltd., Newton Abbot, England

THE BIG BIG BIG BOAT
©1993 by Christine Harder Tangvald for text and Patrick Girouard for illustrations

Designed by Elizabeth A. Thompson
First Printing, 1993
Printed in Singapore
97 96 95 94 93   5 4 3 2 1

Library of Congress Cataloging-in-Publication Data
Tangvald, Christine Harder
        The big big big boat, and other Bible stories about obedience/Christine Harder Tangvald; illustrated by Patrick Girouard.
        p. cm. — (Read aloud, read alone)
        Summary: Simple retellings of three Bible stories that tell how Noah, Moses, and Joshua obeyed God.
        ISBN 0-7814-0926-8
        1. Obedience—biblical teaching—juvenile literature. 2. Noah (biblical figure)—juvenile literature. 3. Moses (biblical leader)—juvenile literature. 4. Joshua (biblical figure)—juvenile literature. 5. Bible stories, English—O.T. [1. Bible stories—O.T. 2. Obedience—biblical teaching. 3. Noah (biblical figure) 4. Moses (biblical leader) 5. Joshua (biblical figure)]
I. Girouard, Patrick, ill. II. Title. III. Series: Tangvald, Christine Harder, Read aloud, read alone.
BS1199.O33T366 1993
222'.109505—dc20   93-9234
                                                                   CIP
                                                                   AC

All Scripture quotations in this publication are from the Holy Bible, New International Version. Copyright © 1973, 1978, 1984, International Bible Society.

THE
BIG BIG BIG
BOAT

Noah **OBEYS** God

"Noah," said God.

"Yes, God," said Noah.

"I want you to build me a boat—
a BIG BIG BIG BIG boat!" said God.

"What for?" asked Noah.

"A flood is coming," said God. "A BIG BIG
flood.

"I need a BIG BIG boat to hold My animals and your family," said God.

"Okay," said Noah. "I will do it! I will build Your BIG BIG boat."

BANG, BANG, BANG!

Hammer, hammer, hammer!

SAW, SAW, SAW!

"What are you doing?"
asked all the other people.
"I am building a BIG
BIG boat," said Noah.
"Why?" asked all the other people.
"Because God told me to. That's why!"
said Noah.

BANG, BANG, BANG!
Hammer, hammer, hammer!
SAW, SAW, SAW!

5

"Ha! Ha! Ha!" said all the other people.

"Look at silly Noah. He is building a silly boat!

Ha! Ha! Ha!"

But Noah just kept on building.

BANG, BANG, BANG!

Hammer, hammer, hammer!

SAW, SAW, SAW!

"Now what are you doing?"
asked all the other people.
"I am putting God's animals
on the boat," said Noah.
"Why?" asked all the other people.
"Because God told me to. That's why,"
said Noah.

"MOO, MOO, MOO,"
went the cows.
"*Hiss, hiss, hiss,*"
went the snakes.
"ROAR, ROAR, ROAR!"
went the lions.
"Ha! Ha! Ha!" said all the other people.
"Look at silly Noah.
Ha! Ha! Ha!"

Noah just kept on loading the animals.

UP, UP, UP went all the animals

of the world . . . two by two.

UP, UP, UP went Mr. and Mrs. Monkey.

UP, UP, UP went Mr. and Mrs. Giraffe.

UP, UP, UP went Mr. and Mrs. Buzzard.

UP into the big big boat.

Then Noah and his family went

UP, UP, UP into the big big boat.

God closed the door.

They waited. They waited and waited.

They waited and waited and waited.

Suddenly . . .

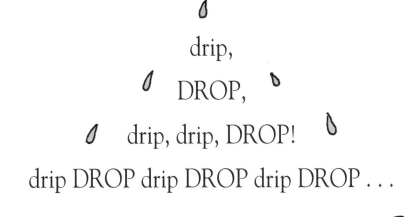

drip,

DROP,

drip, drip, DROP!

drip DROP drip DROP drip DROP . . .

SPLASH!

The rain poured down and the flood came up.

RAIN, RAIN, RAIN, RAIN, RAIN!

For forty days and forty nights it rained.

RAIN, RAIN, RAIN, RAIN, RAIN!

Swoosh . . . whoosh!

The whole wide world was flooded.

But Noah and his family were safe and cozy
inside the BIG BIG boat with all of God's
animals . . . because Noah had OBEYED God.

"MOO, MOO, MOO," said the cows.

"*Hiss, hiss, hiss,*" said the snakes.

"ROAR, ROAR, ROAR!" said the lions.

DOWN, DOWN, DOWN
came Mr. and Mrs. Monkey.
DOWN, DOWN, DOWN
came Mr. and Mrs. Giraffe.
DOWN, DOWN, DOWN
came Mr. and Mrs. Buzzard.
DOWN came all of God's
animals, two by two.

"Hooray, hooray!"
said Noah's family.
"Hooray for Noah!
Hooray for God!"
"Good job, Noah," said God.
"Thanks, God," said Noah.
"I'm glad I OBEYED You."
"So am I," said God. "So am I."

You can find Noah's story in your very own Bible. Ask a grown-up to read it with you. **Genesis 6:9—9:17**.

FIRE, FIRE, FIRE

Moses **OBEYS** God

Oh, my! Oh, dear!
You won't believe what happened to
Moses one day.
It all started when Moses was watching his
sheep—"*Baa, baa, baa*"—
just as he did every day. "*Baa, Baa, Baa.*"

All of a sudden . . .

POOF!

Right before Moses' eyes a
bush burst into flames.
Moses was just about to yell, "FIRE! FIRE!
FIRE!" when he heard a voice.
The voice came right out of the burning bush.
"MOSES, MOSES," said the voice.
"Who is that?" asked Moses. "Who is talking?"
"I AM GOD," said the voice.
"God? Really?" said Moses. "WOW!"

"Moses, I have a job for you. A very important job," said God.

"What is it?" asked Moses.

The bush kept right on burning.

"The evil evil king will not let my people go home to the land I will give them," said God.

"I want you to go to the evil king and tell him to LET MY PEOPLE GO."

"I can't do that," said Moses. "That job is too hard. It is too hard for me. You will have to find someone else."

"I will help you, Moses," said God.

"I will give you power."

"How?" asked Moses. "How can You help me?

How can You give me power?"

The bush kept on burning.

"I will show you," said God.

"Throw your stick onto the ground."

Moses OBEYED God.

He threw his stick onto the ground.

WIGGLE, WIGGLE, WIGGLE!

Slither, slither, slither!

"OH, MY!" yelled Moses. "WATCH OUT!

My stick turned into a real, live snake!"

WIGGLE, WIGGLE, WIGGLE!

Slither, slither, slither!

"Now pick up the snake by its tail," said God.

"By its tail? *Ooooh, ick!*" said Moses.

But he did what God told him to.

He picked up that wiggly old snake by its tail.

GUESS WHAT?

That snake turned right back into a stick!

"WOW! THAT WAS GREAT!" said Moses.

"But I still cannot do Your important job.

You will have to find somebody else."

The bush just kept on burning.

Then God said, "Moses, put your hand inside your robe."

Moses put his hand inside his robe.

When he pulled it out—oh, no! His hand was all covered with horrid ugly terrible sores.

"OH, OH, OH!" said Moses.

"OH, DEAR! THIS IS AWFUL!"

"Put your hand back inside your robe, Moses," said God.

As fast as he could, Moses put his hand back inside his robe.

And GUESS WHAT? No more sores.

"WOW!" said Moses.

"All the sores are gone. That is amazing!"

The bush kept on burning.

"See, I will help you, Moses," said God.

"I will be with you, and I will give you power.

Now, go, Moses.

Take your stick, and

go lead My people to their new home."

"Okay, God," said Moses. "Now I can do it.

Now I WILL do it. I will OBEY You.

I will take my stick, and

I will lead Your people to

their new home."

AND HE DID.

You can find Moses' story in your very own Bible. Ask a grown-up to read it with you. **Exodus 3—4:17.**

MARCH, MARCH, MARCH

Joshua **OBEYS** God

"Joshua," said God.

"Yes, God," said Joshua.

"I have a job for you. A *very important* job," said God.

"What is it?" asked Joshua.

"I want you and My people to march around and around the big bad city of Jericho for seven days," said God.

"I want you to march around and around the city and blow your trumpets."

"You want us to blow our trumpets?" asked Joshua.

"Yes," said God. "BLOW THEM LOUD!"

"Okay, God," said Joshua. "We will do it."

MARCH, MARCH, MARCH!

TROMP, TROMP, TROMP!

STOMP, STOMP, STOMP!

Joshua and God's people marched around the high high walls of the big bad city.

Ta-toot! Ta-toot! Ta-toot! went their trumpets.

"What is Joshua doing?" asked all the people in the big bad city.

"Why is he marching around and around our high high walls?" they asked each other.

Joshua and God's people just kept on marching.

MARCH, MARCH, MARCH!

TROMP, TROMP, TROMP!

STOMP, STOMP, STOMP!

went Joshua and all of God's people.

"HA! HA! HA! HO! HO! HO! Look at silly Joshua," said all the people of the big bad city. "Does he think our high walls will come tumbling down just because he marches around and around on the outside?

"HA! HA! HA! HO! HO! HO!

Look at silly Joshua."

But Joshua and God's people kept right on marching day after day.

MARCH, MARCH, MARCH!

TROMP, TROMP, TROMP!

STOMP, STOMP, STOMP!

Ta-toot! Ta-toot! Ta-toot!

And day after day the people in the big bad city
kept laughing. "HA! HA! HA! HO! HO! HO!
Look at silly, silly Joshua!"

For seven days Joshua marched.

TROMP, TROMP, TROMP!

STOMP, STOMP, STOMP!

For seven days the people of Jericho laughed.

"HA! HA! HA! HO! HO! HO!"

But then . . . on the seventh day . . .

from the very, very top of the high, high wall . . .

tumble, tumble bounce.

Down came one little rock.

Then . . . tumble, bumble, bounce.

Down came a bigger rock.

Then . . . tumble, rumble, CRASH
rumble, crumble, BASH . . . SMASH!
Down, down, down came the high high walls of
the big bad city of Jericho.

"HELP! HELP!" shouted all the people of the big bad city.

"What is happening?" they cried as Joshua and all of God's people charged inside.

"HOORAY! HOORAY!" shouted all of God's people.

"HOORAY for Joshua! HOORAY for God."

"Good job, Joshua," said God.

"Thanks, God," said Joshua. "I am glad we did what You told us to.

I am glad we OBEYED You. I am VERY, VERY glad," said Joshua.

"So am I," said God. "So am I."

You can find Joshua's story in your very own Bible. Ask a grown-up to read it with you. **Joshua 5:13—6:23.**

LET'S TALK ABOUT IT!

After you read the stories, talk about them with a grown-up.

> *If anyone loves me, he will* **OBEY** *my teaching.*
>
> John 14:23a

- What did God ask Noah to do? Did he do it?
- What did God ask Moses to do? Did he do it?
- What did God ask Joshua to do? Did he do it?

WOW! God gave these three men some really big jobs to do, didn't He? Did these three men **OBEY** God? How do you know?

Our Bible verse says if you love God, you will **OBEY** Him, too.
What are some kid-sized ways you can obey God
     —when you are at home?
     —when you are with your friends?
     —when you are at school?

It makes God so happy when you **OBEY** His Word.
     Hooray for Noah!
          Hooray for Joshua!
               Hooray for Moses!
                    . . . and hooray for YOU!